UNDERSTANDING
CHRISTIANITY

BY VALERIE BODDEN

CONTENT CONSULTANT

Scott Moringiello

Assistant Professor
Department of Catholic Studies
DePaul University

Essential Library

An Imprint of Abdo Publishing | abdopublishing.com

UNDERSTANDING
WORLD RELIGIONS
AND BELIEFS

ABDOPUBLISHING.COM

Published by Abdo Publishing, a division of ABDO, PO Box 398166, Minneapolis, Minnesota 55439. Copyright © 2019 by Abdo Consulting Group, Inc. International copyrights reserved in all countries. No part of this book may be reproduced in any form without written permission from the publisher. Essential Library™ is a trademark and logo of Abdo Publishing.

Printed in the United States of America, North Mankato, Minnesota
042018
092018

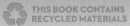
THIS BOOK CONTAINS RECYCLED MATERIALS

Cover Photo: iStockphoto
Interior Photos: Amir Makar/AFP/Getty Images, 4–5; Bikas Das/AP Images, 7; Leonid Andronov/Shutterstock Images, 12–13; Zvonimir Atletic/Shutterstock Images, 14; iStockphoto, 18, 36–37, 41, 48, 51 (top left), 80; Wolfgang Kluge/picture-alliance/dpa/AP Images, 22; Mark Schwettmann/Shutterstock Images, 24–25; Carole Alfarah/Polaris/Newscom, 27; Red Line Editorial, 29; Godong/UIG Universal Images Group/Newscom, 30; Aisha Sultan/TNS/Newscom, 35; Yves Grau/iStockphoto, 39; AR Pictures/Shutterstock Images, 46–47; Chip Studio/iStockphoto, 51 (bottom left), 51 (top right), 51 (bottom right); Clarence Tabb Jr./Detroit News/AP Images, 53; Creative Touch Imaging Ltd./NurPhoto/Getty Images, 56; Giulio Napolitano/Shutterstock Images, 58–59; Jack Kurtz/ZUMA Press/Newscom, 62; Shutterstock Images, 64; Andrii Lutsyk/Shutterstock Images, 68–69; Balazs Mohai/MTI/AP Images, 72; Vitaliy Belousov/Sputnik/AP Images, 74–75; Lobanov Yury/Shutterstock Images, 76; Erika Cross/Shutterstock images, 78–79; Monica Herndon/ZumaPress/Newscom, 84–85; David Massey/Daytona Beach News-Journal/AP Images, 86; Mark Anthony Ray/Shutterstock Images, 90–91; Wolfram Kastl/picture-alliance/dpa/AP Images, 94; Gregorio B. Dantes Jr./Pacific Press/LightRocket/Getty Images, 98

Editor: Marie Pearson
Series Designer: Maggie Villaume

LIBRARY OF CONGRESS CONTROL NUMBER: 2017961380

PUBLISHER'S CATALOGING-IN-PUBLICATION DATA

Name: Bodden, Valerie, author.
Title: Understanding Christianity / by Valerie Bodden.
Description: Minneapolis, Minnesota : Abdo Publishing, 2019. | Series: Understanding world religions and beliefs | Includes online resources and index.
Identifiers: ISBN 9781532114243 (lib.bdg.) | ISBN 9781532154072 (ebook)
Subjects: LCSH: Christianity--Doctrines--Juvenile literature. | Christianity and culture--Juvenile literature. | World religions--Juvenile literature. | Religious belief--Juvenile literature.
Classification: DDC 270.0--dc23

CONTENTS

HE IS RISEN

After the sun set, people in towns and cities across Greece threaded through the dark toward their local Orthodox Church. Many of the churches were decorated with rosemary, a sign of remembrance. Strings of lights and Greek flags hung in others. As the people filed into the church, each carried a white candle. Many wore at least one new item of clothing bought for the occasion. It was Holy Saturday, the night before Easter, when Christians around the world celebrate the resurrection, or return to life, of Jesus Christ.

As time passed, the lights in the church dimmed. Soon, only a single oil lamp at the front of the church lit the building. At midnight, a set of doors in an elaborately decorated wall at the front of the church opened, revealing the altar. A priest passed through the gates carrying a lighted candle. He used it to light one attendee's candle. The attendee, in turn, lit another's candle. In this way, the flame made its way through the church until everyone held a lit candle. The priest then led the people in a procession around the church, reenacting

Worshippers burn candles on Easter to represent Jesus Christ, who is called the light of the world.

the journey of the women who traveled to Jesus's grave the first Easter and found it empty. The congregation filed out of the church, where the priest joyously declared, "Jesus has risen." When the people filed back into the church, the lights blazed, signifying Christ's triumph over death.

After the service, people carried their still-lit candles home. Along the way, they greeted one another with the words, "Christ has risen." Their friends responded, "He has truly risen."[1] Fireworks, car horns, and church bells raised a clamor in the streets. People returned home to a late-night feast that might have included a red Easter egg blessed during the service. Later in the day, many would return to church for another Easter service. After, families would enjoy feasts of roast lamb, sweet braided bread called *tsoureki*, roast chicken, and stuffed grape leaves.

Easter around the World

Christians in Greece are among the more than two billion Christians who celebrate Easter every year.[2] Many celebrate at sunrise services instead of during the night. Some of these services are outdoors. In the Democratic Republic of the Congo, Christians

WHAT'S IN A NAME?

The name Easter comes from an old spring festival called *eastre* in Old English. But in much of the world, Easter goes by another name. In Greek, the holiday is known as *Pasch*, taken from the Hebrew word *Pesach*, or Passover. This is because the first Easter occurred during Passover, a Jewish festival that celebrates how God led his people from slavery in Egypt. In most countries, the name for the celebration of Jesus's resurrection is derived from the Greek word *Pasch*.

Christians in India gather at cemeteries before the sun comes up on Easter.

gather at dawn along the banks of rivers and lakes. Many are dunked under the water in baptism as part of the Easter service. In India, Christians gather early in the morning at the graves of family members who have died. They place small candles on tombs they decorated and whitewashed the previous day. They give thanks that Jesus's resurrection gives their loved ones the promise of Heaven.

In Guatemala, Easter culminates in a week of processions and celebrations. Confetti falls as men and women make their way through the streets carrying heavy floats topped with religious statues. They walk across carpets of colored sawdust, sand, and flower petals arranged into elaborate designs. Firecrackers pop in the air.

Meanwhile, it is quiet in Poland, where church bells have been silent since Maundy Thursday, the Thursday before Easter when Christians remember the Last Supper of Jesus Christ. The bells finally ring out again on Easter. Firecrackers join the bell ringing as a symbol of Jesus bursting from his tomb. People greet one another, saying, "Alleluia."[3] Alleluia means "praise to the Lord." People hurry home to celebrate with a feast after church services, enjoying meat and other foods that they did not often eat during the 40 days of their Lenten fast.

THE WEEK BEFORE EASTER

Christians call the week before Easter Holy Week. Special days recall significant events in the last week of Jesus's life. Palm Sunday is the Sunday before Easter, marking the day Jesus rode into Jerusalem on a donkey. He was greeted joyously, and people placed palm branches on the ground in front of him. Maundy Thursday, or Holy Thursday, is the night Jesus celebrated the Last Supper with his disciples. He held the first Holy Communion when he gave them bread and wine, which he said were his body and blood. Good Friday is the day on which Jesus was crucified. Easter Sunday is the day Jesus rose from the dead.

In Rome, 80,000 people crowd into Saint Peter's Square.[4] They listen in reverence as the pope, the leader of the Roman Catholic Church, leads an outdoor service on the steps leading into Saint Peter's Basilica. The pope then delivers a message of peace and hope to the world. Many more Catholics listen to the message on television, as do other Christians and non-Christians.

In the United States, Christians fill churches, mountaintops, beaches, parks, gymnasiums, and storefronts for dawn services. Some gatherings are small, while buses and shuttles carry thousands of people to others. Music ranges from traditional hymns to gospel choirs and modern praise bands playing rock-inspired songs. Many congregations come together for an Easter breakfast after the service.

In China, where many forms of Christianity are illegal, people may gather in secret for Easter worship. Some Christians worship in small house churches. Others travel to services at priests' homes, where crowds may grow so large they overflow the building and spill into alleys and onto rooftops. Despite the risk of punishment, they pray and sing along with songs played on bugles and metal drums.

The Easter Story

Although it is celebrated differently around the world, Easter is recognized by Christians everywhere as the most important festival of the year. The holiday centers on the heart of the Christian faith—the death and resurrection of Jesus, the Son of God.

ROVING EASTER

Unlike many holidays, Easter is not celebrated on the same date every year. Because the first Easter occurred during the seven-day Jewish Passover, the date for Easter is based on the date of Passover. Passover begins on the first full moon after the spring equinox. Because the first Easter occurred on a Sunday, Easter is always on a Sunday. So Easter is always on the first Sunday following the first full moon after the spring equinox. It can fall anytime between March 22 and April 25. But the Eastern Orthodox Church uses a different calendar. In some years, Eastern Orthodox Christians celebrate Easter on the same date as Western Christians. In other years, Eastern Orthodox Easter occurs a week or more after Easter in the West.

According to the Bible, Jesus was crucified, or killed by hanging on a cross, on a Friday—a day now known as Good Friday. Jesus had predicted he would rise from the dead, so his enemies convinced the Roman governors to seal the tomb with a large stone and place guards in front of it. When his followers returned to Jesus's tomb three days after his death, on Easter Sunday, they found the stone rolled away. Jesus's body was gone. Angels announced that Jesus had risen from the dead. Afterward, Jesus appeared to his disciples, or followers, on several occasions. He promised that they, too, would be resurrected one day. He commanded his disciples to share his message with the world. After 40 days, he ascended into Heaven.

From its small beginnings, Christianity has grown into one of the world's major religions and has reached nearly every part of the globe. In some

PASSION PLAYS

The Romans reserved crucifixion for the worst criminals. First, criminals were beaten with sharp whips. Then their hands and feet were nailed or tied to wooden crosses that were raised upright in the ground. Hanging from their wrists and feet, criminals could not breathe unless they pushed up against the bindings or nails. They might spend hours or days on the cross until they grew too exhausted to push. As they sagged forward, blood flow and air supply were cut off, resulting in a slow, painful death.

Jesus's suffering and death are often called his passion, from the Latin word *passio*, or "suffer." Since the Middle Ages (476–1400s), Christians have held passion plays to reenact the story of Jesus's crucifixion, burial, and resurrection. The 2004 film *The Passion of the Christ* is one famous passion play. Although condemned by some for its violence, the film earned praise for its realistic depiction of Jesus's suffering before and during his crucifixion. It became the most successful independent film of all time, earning more than $600 million at the box office.[6] In 2016, *Passion* screenwriter Randall Wallace said a sequel based on Jesus's resurrection was in the works. "The *Passion* is the beginning and there's a lot more story to tell," he said.[7]

countries, the majority of people are Christian, while in others Christians are only a small minority. Although Christians today follow many different traditions and practices, they are linked by belief in Jesus's resurrection. Presbyterian Pastor Enock De Assis said, "The cornerstone of the Christian faith is the resurrection of Christ. If there was no resurrection, there would be no Christianity. . . . We have different theologies and different liturgies, but there is one thing that unites all the Christians around the world and that is Christ is risen."[5]

Bethlehem is located in what is now Palestine.

CHAPTER TWO

IN THE BEGINNING

Christianity has its roots in Judaism. In ancient times, the Jewish people lived in a region along the eastern Mediterranean Sea that includes present-day Palestinian territories and Israel.

Several foreign powers had ruled this region by the time of Jesus's birth. The most recent was the Romans, who took control of Palestine in 63 BCE. The Jews looked forward to the coming of a Messiah, about whom the Hebrew Bible prophesied, or foretold. The word *Messiah*, or *Christos* (Christ) in Greek, means "anointed one." The term refers to the practice of anointing the head of a new king with oil. Some Jews believed the Messiah would be a king who would free them from Roman rule. Others looked for a spiritual Messiah.

Christians believe that Jesus of Nazareth, who was born in the town of Bethlehem sometime between the years 6 and 4 BCE, was God's Son and the long-awaited Messiah. Jesus did not come

Many artists have depicted
Jesus's crucifixion.

to free people from oppression on Earth. Instead, he came to save them from sin.

When he was approximately 30 years old, Jesus began traveling throughout Palestine, preaching and teaching. He performed many miracles. He healed the sick, restored sight to the blind, and even raised people from the dead. Many people believed Jesus was the Messiah and followed him. His closest followers, including Peter, James, and John, came to be known as his 12 disciples or 12 apostles. But others, including Jewish religious leaders, were angry of the attention Jesus received. They saw Jesus's claim to be God as blasphemy.

Jesus preached for three years before Jewish leaders and the Roman government had him crucified. He rose from the dead three days later. Jesus remained among his disciples and appeared to others for a short time before ascending into Heaven.

Into the World

Jesus commanded his disciples to share the Gospel—Greek for "good news"—of his resurrection. They spread the Christian religion throughout the known world, including to Gentile, or non-Jewish, people. Word of Jesus's resurrection quickly spread throughout Asia Minor—present-day Turkey—and other parts of the Roman Empire. Although the Romans welcomed people worshipping many gods into the empire, early Christians often faced death and persecution. The Romans feared

PERSPECTIVES

SAINT PAUL

Saul of Tarsus, later known as Paul, was born in approximately 4 BCE in present-day Turkey. He was a Pharisee, a Jewish leader educated in Jewish traditions and law. As a young man, Paul gained a reputation for persecuting Christians, whom he viewed as heretics. He wrote of his life as a Pharisee: "For you have heard of my previous way of life in Judaism, how intensely I persecuted the church of God and tried to destroy it. I was advancing in Judaism beyond many of my own age among my people and was extremely zealous for the traditions of my fathers."[1]

Paul had a dramatic experience in approximately 33 CE. While on the way to Damascus, he had a vision in which Christ revealed himself. As Paul recounted, "The gospel I preached is not of human origin. I did not receive it from any man, nor was I taught it; rather, I received it by revelation from Jesus Christ."[2] After receiving this revelation, Paul became a missionary, starting churches throughout Asia Minor and parts of Europe. Of the 27 books in the New Testament, Paul is credited with authoring 13.[3] He is believed to have been martyred in Rome sometime between 62 and 64 CE.

MARTYRS

Before Constantine legalized Christianity in the Roman Empire, many Christians faced persecution and even martyrdom, or death for their faith. Most of Jesus's 12 disciples were martyred. Christians who refused to offer sacrifices to the Roman gods were often executed. Christians still face martyrdom today. More Christians were killed in the 1900s than in the 400 years of Roman rule that followed Jesus's resurrection. Modern-day Christians have been martyred in North Korea, Saudi Arabia, Somalia, India, and other locations across the globe.

that the Christians' refusal to offer sacrifices to the Roman gods and to the emperor would anger the gods and endanger the empire.

The situation for Christians improved in 313 CE, when Roman emperor Constantine issued the Edict of Milan, which legalized Christianity. Over time, Christianity became not only accepted but also favored. In 381 CE, Emperor Theodosius made it the official religion of the Roman Empire.

After Christianity was legalized, some people became Christian to gain favor within the Roman Empire. In response, some Christian men who were dedicated to living a godly life moved away from society to spend their time in prayer. These were the first monks, and many lived in complete seclusion. Over time, groups of monks came together to form monasteries, where they dedicated themselves to prayer and worship. Many monasteries also cared for the poor and sick in nearby communities. Some Christian women did the same. They became nuns, lived in convents, and devoted themselves to God and to caring for others.

Making It Official

As Christianity spread, theologians found they needed a clear definition of the religion's doctrines, or core beliefs. These doctrines would help them communicate the true nature of God and especially of Christ. Official doctrines would also counter heresies, or beliefs that contradict Christian teachings, that had sprung up among some believers.

To define these doctrines, church leaders from around the world gathered for a number of councils. In 325 CE, leaders at the Council of Nicaea discussed the true nature of Jesus Christ. They condemned the heresy that Jesus was not divine and insisted that he was both God and man. The Council of Constantinople in 381 continued the work of the Council of Nicaea. It confirmed the doctrine of the Trinity, a belief that God is one God but three persons—Father, Son, and Holy Spirit. The council formulated Christian doctrine into a creed, or statement of beliefs, known as the Nicene Creed. Christians in many churches still recite this creed today. In 451, the Council of Chalcedon reaffirmed the belief that Christ was both true God and true man.

During the early centuries of the Christian church, various letters and books written by the apostles were circulated to teach the Christian faith. Many of these works were regarded by early Christians as inspired, or directly influenced, by God. Over time, the inspired writings were included in the canon, or official scriptures, of the church. The church canon was largely agreed upon by the late 300s.

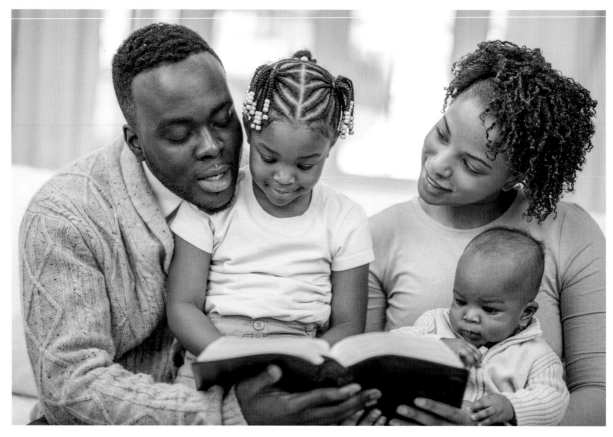

Inspired letters and books written by the apostles can be found in the Christian Bible.

Division in the Church

The Roman Empire fell in the West in 476. It continued in the East as the Byzantine Empire, with its capital in Constantinople. Gradually, the churches in the East and the West divided over their practices and organizations. Differences in language further separated the churches. Those in the West spoke Latin, while the language of the Eastern churches was largely Greek.

The greatest disputes arose over the role of the bishop of Rome, also known as the pope. Some churches in the East resented the claim that the pope was the head of all bishops. The final disagreement between the East and the West occurred over the wording of the Nicene Creed. The version of the creed agreed upon at the Council of Constantinople said the Holy Spirit proceeds, or comes, from the Father. But the Western church later added the words "and the Son," a phrase known in Latin as the *filioque*. The Eastern church saw the filioque as theologically incorrect. The church in the East also resented the fact that the Western church had changed the creed without consulting the entire church body. In 1054, disagreements over the filioque and other issues led to a split between the Eastern Orthodox Church and the Western Roman Catholic Church.

Violent Years

Meanwhile, the religion Islam had spread rapidly through Palestine, Egypt, and Syria. Muslims took over Jerusalem and other lands considered holy to Christians. In 1095, Pope Urban II sent out the first crusaders. These fighters were on a mission to retake the Holy Land. Although the primary goal of the Crusades was to overcome the Muslims, crusaders also directed their wrath against Jewish people. Many Christians believed the Jews had been responsible for Jesus's death and therefore had been rejected by God. Thousands of Muslim and Jewish men, women, and children were killed throughout the First Crusade and its aftermath. The First Crusade came to an end in 1099 with the fall of Jerusalem to the crusaders. But the Holy Land was soon retaken by the Muslims, and further Crusades in 1147, 1189, and 1202 failed to restore the Holy Land to Christian control.

The Crusades exposed the people of Europe to new ideas and practices, leading some to adopt beliefs considered heretical. Some, for example, embraced the idea of reincarnation, or being reborn into a new body after death. The Roman Catholic Church sought to eliminate these beliefs through the Inquisition. Groups of inquisitors investigated claims of heresy. Those found guilty might have to complete a simple penance, or punishment, such as saying a certain number of prayers or fasting. Others faced loss of property, life in prison, or death. In some places, the Inquisition also targeted Jews and Muslims, who were forced to wear items that set them apart, such as pointed hats or yellow badges.

The Reformation

By the early 1500s, some theological leaders were concerned with the practices of the Western church. Among them was Martin Luther, a German monk who feared he would never be able to live up to God's standards. Luther dedicated himself to studying the Bible while serving as a professor at the University of Wittenberg in Germany. What he found convinced him that his ideas about salvation, or how to be saved from sin, were wrong. He had always believed the church's doctrine that he had to participate in earning his salvation by doing good works. But Luther came to see that wasn't true. Good works would never be enough to erase people's sin. Instead, God justified them, or declared

THE PRINTING PRESS AND PROTESTANTISM

Bibles can be found almost everywhere today, from bookstores to hotel rooms, as well as online and as apps. But early believers of Christianity did not have such easy access to the Bible. Until the invention of the printing press in the 1400s, books were handwritten. This was often done by monks, who spent their days carefully copying scripture. Even when books were available, few people could read. Instead, they learned Bible stories through church services and the stained glass windows and artwork that decorated local churches. Dramas and songs helped to reinforce the messages.

The invention of moveable-type printing presses in 1454 helped spread the ideas of the Protestant Reformation quickly. Literacy levels rose, and more people could own Bibles. Protestant reformers encouraged those who could read to study God's word for themselves rather than rely on the church to interpret it for them.

them innocent of their sins. This was a gift of grace, or undeserved love, given freely by God through the death of Jesus Christ. Luther believed that justification came only through faith in God. The basis of this faith was the Bible alone, not church tradition.

Luther was also alarmed by some of the practices of the Roman Catholic Church, including the selling of indulgences. These were certificates that promised to apply the extra merits, or good works, of saints to souls in purgatory. Purgatory was believed to be a period of punishment that purified the dead for entry into Heaven. Indulgences were supposed to help reduce the time a soul

spent in purgatory. People could buy indulgences to benefit themselves or others already in purgatory. Indulgence sales funded the building of cathedrals, including the Cathedral of Saint Peter in Rome.

Luther documented his concerns in the Ninety-Five Theses, which he posted on the church door in Wittenberg, Germany, on October 31, 1517. Luther wanted to spur public debate. But church leaders called Luther's statements heresy and insisted that he recant, or take back, his theses. He refused. Although he had simply wanted to reform the church, Luther sparked what came to be known as the Protestant Reformation.

Visitors to Wittenberg can visit the church where Luther posted his Ninety-Five Theses.

He was joined by several other reformers. Over time, the Reformation led to the establishment of several non-Catholic, or Protestant, denominations.

Following the Protestant Reformation, the Roman Catholic Church went through a period of reform known as the Counter-Reformation. The Council of Trent, a series of meetings held between 1545 and 1563, ended the abuse of indulgences. It also formed measures to stem corruption among clergy and to ensure priests were well trained in the scriptures. At the same time, the Council of Trent reaffirmed the Roman Catholic Church's core beliefs. These beliefs include the equal authority of scripture and church tradition, as well as the doctrine that people are saved by both faith and good works. The Counter-Reformation led to renewed efforts by the Roman Catholic Church to spread the Gospel around the world.

CHRISTIANS AND THE HOLOCAUST

By the time of the Reformation, anti-Semitism—or anti-Jewish feelings—had dominated Europe for more than 1,000 years. Many European Christians blamed the Jews for killing Jesus. Others resented Jews who had become successful businesspeople. In some places, Jews were forced to live in separate areas of cities known as ghettos. In his early years as a reformer, Luther attempted to convert many Jews to Christianity. When they refused to convert, Luther expressed strongly anti-Semitic views. In the 1930s and 1940s, German leader Adolf Hitler used some of these views to justify his actions in persecuting Jews and sending them to labor camps. He took anti-Semitism even further, killing an estimated six million Jews during the Holocaust.[4] Today, many Christians reject anti-Semitic views, and many church bodies have issued apologies for Christians' role in the Holocaust.

CHRISTIANITY AROUND THE WORLD

Today, Christianity is the largest religion in the world. Around the world, 2.3 billion people, approximately one-third of the world's population, practice Christianity.[1] Approximately one-half of all Christians belong to the Roman Catholic Church. Another 37 percent are Protestant, while 12 percent are Orthodox.[2]

Spreading God's Word

Christianity has its roots in the Middle East. The first missionaries—people assigned to bring God's word to non-Christians—traveled from there to share the message of Christ's resurrection with people in Europe, Africa, and Asia Minor. Europe quickly became the new center of Christianity, and, for more than 1,000 years, most of the world's Christians lived there.

Christian influence can be found around the world. Visitors can see the Christ the Redeemer statue in Rio de Janeiro, Brazil.

During the late 1400s and early 1500s, European explorers set out to discover new lands. Their crews often included at least one or two missionaries, who were assigned to work with the indigenous peoples. In some cases, colonial powers forced indigenous peoples to convert to Christianity. From the mid-1800s to the late 1900s in North America, for example, many American Indian children were forcibly removed from their families and placed in boarding schools. They were forced to convert to Christianity and adopt the clothing, language, and other aspects of white American or Canadian culture.

Today's missionaries continue to travel to speak with people around the world about their beliefs. But many are careful to give people an opportunity to choose to accept the Christian faith. Missionaries work to build positive relationships with local peoples and retain aspects of indigenous cultures that align with Christian beliefs. They recognize that people practice Christianity differently because it exists in diverse regions around the world.

Christianity in the Middle East

In the 600s, Christianity thrived throughout much of the Middle East. But the Arabs from the south and west who conquered the region brought with them a new religion—Islam. The Arabs allowed Christians to continue practicing Christianity, but doing so subjected Christians to double taxes and other restrictions. Some even faced persecution. These hardships led some Christians to convert to Islam. Over time, the Christian population shrank until it was limited to only small, isolated pockets.

Some churches in Lebanon opened their doors to Christian refugees from Syria and Iraq, who fled their homes because of violence and persecution.

Today, Christians in the Middle East are isolated in small minority communities, making up approximately 4 percent of the region's total population. Lebanon has the largest proportion of Christians, with Christians making up as much as 35 percent of the country's population.[3]

Other countries have almost no Christians. This is in part because of laws outlawing the practice of Christianity except in limited cases, such as by foreigners.

Christianity in Africa

Shortly after Jesus's birth, his mother Mary and her husband Joseph fled with him to Egypt to escape the wrath of King Herod. Herod had heard of the promised Messiah and feared the Messiah would take Herod's position as king. To eliminate this threat, Herod ordered all boys in Bethlehem under the age of two killed. Jesus's family eventually moved back to the area. Years later, word of Jesus's death and resurrection spread to Egypt and other parts of North Africa.

Despite Christianity's roots in Africa, the faith did not immediately spread across the continent. The region of Africa south of the Sahara Desert remained largely non-Christian until the 1800s and 1900s, when missionaries brought Christianity to most of the continent. Today, the religion is growing faster in Africa than anywhere else. Approximately 516 million people—or 63 percent of the population—of sub-Saharan Africa is Christian. The continent is home to nearly one-quarter of all Christians in the world.[4] Three African countries—Nigeria, the Democratic Republic of the Congo, and Ethiopia—have some of the largest populations of Christians in the world. Despite the rapid spread of Christianity, some countries in Africa remain almost entirely non-Christian, including Niger, Tunisia, Algeria, and Morocco.

Countries with the Largest Christian Populations[5]		
Country	Number of Christians in 2010	Percentage of World Christian Population
United States	247,000,000	11.3%
Brazil	176,000,000	8%
Mexico	108,000,000	4.9%
Russia	105,000,000	4.8%
Philippines	87,000,000	4%
Nigeria	81,000,000	3.7%
China	67,000,000	3.1%
Democratic Republic of the Congo	63,000,000	2.9%
Germany	58,000,000	2.7%
Ethiopia	53,000,000	2.4%

Nearly half of all Christians in the world live in the ten countries with the largest Christian populations.

Christianity in Asia

According to church tradition, the apostle Thomas spread the Christian message as far east as India before 100 CE. That's why some countries, including Armenia, have large Christian populations. But other countries and cultures haven't always been welcoming. Since as early as the 1500s, the Christian church has been met with government and religious resistance, particularly in countries that practice Hinduism and Confucianism. This continues in some Asian countries even today. In Malaysia, for example, the majority of people are Muslim. Although the word *Allah* is Arabic for "god," it is largely used throughout the world to specifically refer to the Muslim God. Christians in Malaysia have used

The Yoido Full Gospel Church holds services in Korean, English, Indonesian, Chinese, and other languages.

Allah in their Bibles for a long time. But since 2007, Christians are not allowed to use the term outside of church. Some Malaysians say Muslims might get confused and convert to Christianity, which is a crime in certain areas. As a result, the majority of the Bibles used in the country are technically illegal. In other countries, Christians face difficulties in getting approval to build churches. Instead, they meet in houses that are used as churches.

Despite these difficulties, Asia has the second-fastest-growing population of Christians. The number of Christians in Asia reached more than 285 million in 2010. Christians now make up 7 percent of the Asian population.[6] The Philippines has the greatest percentage of Christians on the continent, with almost the whole population belonging to either the Roman Catholic or another Christian church. Christians also make up 29 percent of the South Korean population.[7] Yoido Full Gospel Church in Seoul, South Korea, is the largest church in the world, with 800,000 members.[8]

Nepal and China have the fastest-growing Christian populations in Asia and around the globe. Some scholars believe China will have the largest Christian population in the world by 2030. Because religion of any kind is restricted in China, some Chinese Christians meet secretly in house churches to avoid government persecution. Others attend churches connected to the government-sanctioned Three-Self Patriotic Movement, which the government closely regulates. It focuses on the social benefits of Christianity.

STATE RELIGION

The governments of 43 countries have state, or official, religions. According to the Pew Research Center, "In some cases, state religions have roles that are largely ceremonial."[12] But it also notes that many countries reward those who follow the state religion with low taxes, good financial aid, ease in purchasing property, or other benefits. Countries that do this are likely to restrict or ban the practice of other religions.

Most countries with a state religion are in the Middle East and North Africa, where Islam is the official religion in 27 countries. Christianity is the state religion in 13 countries, mostly in Europe. Judaism is the official religion in Israel, while Buddhism is the state religion of Cambodia and Bhutan. Ten countries, including China, Cuba, North Korea, and Vietnam, tightly regulate or forbid religious practice of any kind.[13]

Christianity in Europe

One hundred years ago, nearly 67 percent of all Christians lived in Europe. Today, only 26 percent of the world's Christian population lives on that continent.[9] Nearly one-half of all European Christians are Roman Catholic. Eighteen percent are Protestant and 35 percent are Orthodox.[10] Roman Catholic Christians tend to be concentrated in western, southern, and central Europe. Protestantism has a strong influence in northern Europe, while Orthodox Christians can be found largely in eastern Europe.

Approximately 76 percent of Europeans identify as Christian.[11] But some European countries are largely secular, meaning that the majority of the population does not belong to any religion. Secular countries include Belgium and the Netherlands. Turkey is the only European country that is almost entirely non-Christian. The majority of its population is Muslim.

Christianity in Latin America

The first Christian service in the Americas was held on the island of Hispaniola on January 6, 1494. It was two years after Christopher Columbus first arrived in the New World. Columbus's expedition was soon followed by those of other Spanish explorers known as conquistadors. The conquistadors quickly enslaved and killed millions of indigenous people. Missionaries traveling with the conquistadors spread Christianity to those who survived the devastation. Millions of indigenous people in Mexico converted to Christianity by the mid-1500s. Elegant cathedrals and monasteries sprang up in Latin American cities.

Over time, diverse Christian traditions took root in Latin America. In Latin America today, 69 percent of people are Roman Catholic.[14] Many practice a form of folk Catholicism that combines traditional beliefs with Roman Catholic teachings. Many Latin American Christians place a heavy emphasis on venerating, or showing reverence for, the saints and especially for Jesus's mother, the Virgin Mary. A shortage of Roman Catholic priests

SANTERIA

In some parts of the world, people have combined Christian practices with other religions. This process is known as syncretism. In Latin America, for example, many people practice Santeria, Spanish for "the way of the saints." This religion has its roots in the African religions brought to Latin America by enslaved peoples. Although Santeria incorporates Christian saints, it identifies those saints with pagan deities, called orishas, who are called upon for protection, wisdom, and success.

in rural areas has led many people to practice *piedad popular*, Spanish for "popular piety." In this type of Catholicism, people do not attend weekly services but instead celebrate occasional festivals, often in honor of a special saint. Each region develops many of its own customs for such celebrations.

NOMINAL CHRISTIANS

Not all Christians actively practice their faith through worship attendance, prayer, or other activities. Some are nominal Christians, or Christians in name only. They may identify as Christians because their families have always been Christian or because they consider themselves good people. In Spain, for example, only 17 percent of those who identify as Roman Catholic attend church on a regular basis. By contrast, more than half of Christians in several African countries, including Zimbabwe and Nigeria, attend weekly worship services.

Christianity in North America

Christianity came to North America with the first European settlers and has since spread across the continent. In Canada, there are more Roman Catholics than Protestants. Meanwhile, more than 46 percent of Americans belong to Protestant denominations, while 20.8 percent are Roman Catholic. Less than 1 percent are Orthodox.[15] Church affiliation varies by region. In the northeastern United States, there are approximately the same number of Roman Catholics and Protestants. The western, midwestern, and southern states, on the other hand, are largely Protestant.

Although Christianity is the majority religion in the United States, the percentage of Americans identifying as Christian fell from 78.4 percent in 2007 to 70.6 percent in 2014. Approximately 2 percent of the US population is Jewish and 1 percent is Muslim. Nearly 23 percent of Americans consider themselves nonreligious.[16]

Some churches have unique designs. Thorncrown Chapel in Arkansas has glass walls.

CHRISTIAN BELIEFS

Although Christians around the world worship in different ways, they are united in their core beliefs. These beliefs are based on the Bible, which Christians believe is God's word. The word *Bible* comes from the Greek word *biblia*, meaning "the books." The Bible is a collection of books written during the course of 1,000 years. It has sold more copies than any other book. The full book has been translated into more than 650 languages, and parts of it have been translated into more than 1,500 languages.[1] It is divided into two parts, or testaments.

The Old Testament is made up of the Jewish scriptures. It includes books that tell the history of God's people, as well as books of poetry and books of prophecy. The Old Testament also lays out laws for God's people. Some of those laws have to do with civil regulations for Jewish society and rituals to be used in Jewish

Some Christians meet regularly to help each other learn about the Bible.

sacrifices and ceremonies. The Ten Commandments are moral laws that set standards of right and wrong. These include the command to worship no other gods. The Ten Commandments forbid murder, adultery, and stealing. The Old Testament promises the coming of a Messiah who will save God's people.

The New Testament tells about the fulfillment of that promised Messiah in Jesus Christ. Four books, known as Gospels, tell of the life, teachings, death, and resurrection of Jesus. The book of Acts describes the activity of the early church immediately following Jesus's resurrection. The New Testament also includes several letters written by apostles to the early churches. Revelation, the final book of the New Testament, provides a vision of the end of the world, when Jesus will return to judge both believers and unbelievers.

Most Christians believe the Bible was inspired by God—that is, God directed or influenced human authors as they wrote his word. Others believe that the Bible's writers had unique spiritual insights but were not led by God in what they wrote. Christians also vary in their view of the Bible's accuracy. Many see the Bible as true and accurate in every aspect. Other Christians believe the Bible is accurate only in essential matters of faith and doctrine.

The Nature of God

Christianity is a monotheistic religion, meaning Christians believe in one God. But they believe God is triune. He is one God in three persons: Father, Son, and Holy Spirit. All three persons of God are equal,

A common symbol of the Holy Spirit is a white dove.

and the Trinity cannot be divided. Yet each person of the Trinity is also distinct. For example, it was God the Son who took on human form in the person of Jesus Christ and died to save humans from their sins. But God the Son cannot be separated from the Father or from the Holy Spirit.

God is all powerful, omnipotent, and eternal. He exists outside of time and space and is not limited by them. At the same time, God is all-loving and present everywhere in the world. He does not control humans as puppets, but he does work out his divine purposes in the world.

ANGELS AND DEMONS

Christians believe that in addition to the visible creation, God also created invisible, spiritual beings called angels. In the Bible, angels sometimes take on human form. They might wear dazzling clothes or be surrounded by bright light. The word *angel* comes from a Greek word meaning "messenger," and this is the role angels often fulfill in the Bible. For example, the angel Gabriel appeared to Mary to announce that she would give birth to the Son of God. Other angels, known as destroying angels, carried out God's judgment on his people when they turned away from him. For example, God sent a destroying angel to kill 70,000 Israelites after their king, David, deliberately defied him.[2]

The spiritual realm also includes demons. Led by Satan, also known as the Devil, these former angels rebelled against God. Demons attempt to lead people away from God. During Jesus's life on Earth, Satan tried unsuccessfully to tempt him to sin. With Jesus's death and resurrection, he overcame Satan's power. Other demons can influence and deceive people, orchestrate evil and death, and cause physical or emotional suffering. However, God has authority over demons, as demons obeyed Jesus in the New Testament.

Sin

God is the standard of perfection. He created a perfect world. But the first humans—Adam and Eve—sinned. Sin is a failure to live up to God's standard of perfection and obey his commands. As a result of Adam and Eve's sin, all of creation was corrupted by evil. Everyone born after Adam and Eve inherited their sinful nature. People were no longer capable of fully obeying God.

God created Adam and Eve without sin. God told them not to eat fruit from the tree of the knowledge of good and evil. But a serpent generally thought to be Satan convinced them to eat the fruit, which brought sin into the world.

The consequence of sin is death—not only physical death but also eternal death in Hell and separation from God. Because of humans' sinful nature, they cannot overcome sin on their own. They need a savior.

In his grace, God sent his son, Jesus, to save people from their sins. Jesus was born of a virgin named Mary. He was both fully human and fully God. Jesus lived a perfect, sinless life. When he died on the cross, he took on the punishment for the sins of the whole world. God counted Jesus's death as paying the penalty for all human sins. As a result, those who have faith in Jesus as their savior no longer have to fear God's judgment. As God punished Jesus for their sins, God will see Jesus's perfection when he judges Christians. Jesus's resurrection from the dead gives believers the promise that they, too, will one day rise from the dead to live with God forever.

Life and Faith

Through his life and teachings, Jesus showed Christians how they were to live. When asked to name the greatest commandment, Jesus replied: "'Love the Lord your God with all your heart and with all your soul and with all your mind.' This is the first and greatest commandment. And the second is like it: 'Love your neighbor as yourself.'"[3] Jesus taught that wrong thoughts were just as sinful as wrong actions. He said, "You have heard that it was said to the people long ago, 'You shall not murder, and anyone who murders will be subject to judgment.' But I tell you that anyone who is angry with a brother or sister will be subject to judgment."[4] Jesus also told Christians to love their enemies and forgive those who hurt them.

Christians know they cannot live up to God's standards because of their own sinful natures. But they believe that through faith they have been given a new life in Christ. They strive to uphold his commands out of love for him. They trust that when they fail and repent—which means to express sorrow for their sin and turn away from it—God forgives them.

Life after Death

Death is not the end for Christians, but beliefs about what happens after it vary. Many believe the soul and body separate at death. Some believe the soul goes directly to Heaven. Some Protestants believe the soul enters a temporary state similar to sleep. Roman Catholics, Orthodox Christians, and some Protestants believe the soul faces immediate judgment and remains in a condition of waiting,

PARABLES

Jesus often taught in parables, or short stories that use images from everyday life to teach deeper spiritual truths. For example, Jesus told a parable about a shepherd who had lost a sheep. Although the shepherd had 99 other sheep, he left them to find his one lost sheep. When he found it, he celebrated with his friends. In the parable, the shepherd stands for Jesus. The sheep are his people. Jesus told this parable to show his desire to reach sinners. He explained, "In the same way, there will be more rejoicing in heaven over one sinner who repents than over ninety-nine righteous persons who do not need to repent."[5]

during which people on Earth can say prayers to benefit the deceased person. For Roman Catholics, the condition of waiting is in purgatory, a place or state in which the soul endures punishment for earthly sins to purify it for entry into Heaven.

Christians look forward to the last day, or final Judgment, spoken of in the book of Revelation. On that day, Jesus will return in glory to raise all people from the dead. People's souls will be reunited with their bodies. Then, Jesus will judge all people. Those who believed in him will spend eternity with him in Heaven.

Christians differ in their beliefs about where or what Heaven is. Some think it is a physical location. Others believe it is a spiritual state of being. Whether a place or a state, most Christians believe that in Heaven they will live forever in the presence of God. There will be no more sin, suffering, or sadness. Some Christians see Heaven as a good quality of life they work to attain on Earth rather than a place they go after death.

Non-Christians will also recognize Jesus for who he really is at the final Judgment. But because they have rejected him, they will spend eternity separated from God. Most Christians believe unbelievers will face punishment in Hell. As with Heaven, some believe Hell is a physical location, while others see it as a state of being. Some Christians do not believe in Hell at all but instead believe God will save all people.

THE PROBLEM OF EVIL

Some people wonder why a good and loving God would allow evil and suffering in the world. If God is all powerful, they wonder, why doesn't he put a stop to everything bad that happens? But Christians believe evil in this world is a result of sin. When Adam and Eve sinned, they corrupted not only human beings but also all of God's creation. As a result of sin, the world faces natural disasters, diseases, and other hardships. While they live on the earth, humans must face the consequences of sin. But someday, Jesus will come back to bring believers with him to Heaven, where there will be no more suffering or death.

The floor in the nave of Saint Peter's Basilica is made mostly of marble.

WORSHIP AND PRAISE

Christians express and practice their faith through worship services. These services are traditionally held on Sundays, but many churches also offer services on Saturday nights or weekdays. The capitalized word *Church* is sometimes used to refer to all Christians everywhere. *Church* comes from the Greek word *kyriakos*, meaning "belonging to the Lord." Although all Christians worship the same God, they do so as part of different congregations, or communities. These congregations meet for worship in a variety of buildings that range from elaborate structures to simple storefronts.

The earliest Christian communities met in house churches, which were sometimes modified to fit large crowds. With the legalization of Christianity throughout the Roman world in 313 CE, worship services moved into basilicas. These long, rectangular buildings were originally used as courtrooms and public marketplaces but

The Hagia Sophia was completed in 537 CE.

were soon built specifically to hold worship services. The nave, or main area, of the basilica was left

open and without seats, as worshippers stood for the entire service. The most famous basilica is Saint

Peter's, which was completed in Rome in 1615 CE. Other early churches, such as the Hagia Sophia in

Constantinople, feature rounded domes and arched windows and doorways.

FESTIVALS AND HOLIDAYS

In addition to regular weekly worship services, Christians also celebrate several festivals and holidays throughout the year. The cycle of festivals observed by the church every year is referred to as the liturgical, or church, year. It begins four Sundays before Christmas with the season of Advent. Advent means "coming." During this time, Christians look forward to the celebration of Christ's birth at Christmas. They also look to his second coming, when he will return to judge believers and unbelievers.

Although no one knows the exact day on which Jesus was born, most Christians celebrate his birth on December 25 each year. Some Orthodox Christians celebrate Christmas on January 7. Christmas is followed by Epiphany in January. This festival commemorates the arrival of magi, or wise men, from the East who visited Jesus after his birth. In Eastern Orthodox churches, Epiphany celebrates Jesus's baptism.

In late winter, Christians observe Lent, a somber 40-day period of reflection and repentance in preparation for Easter. Forty days after Easter, they recall Jesus's return to Heaven in the festival of Ascension. Ten days later is Pentecost, a celebration of the coming of the Holy Spirit to believers.

By the mid-1100s, church architecture was dominated by a new style known as Gothic. Large Gothic cathedrals featured pointed arches, towering pinnacles, and stained glass windows that allowed multicolored light to filter into the building. The best-known Gothic-style cathedral is Notre Dame in Paris, France, begun in 1163.

After the Reformation, some churches, especially those established later on in the United States, took on a simpler form. Early Protestant churches might have had a single steeple, or tower, rather than multiple pinnacles. Because teaching was a prominent part of Protestant worship, the inside of Protestant churches generally included pews, or benches. These allowed worshippers to sit while listening to someone teach about the Bible.

CHRISTIAN SYMBOLS

Christians use many symbols to represent their faith. Today, these symbols can be found on everything from church decorations and stained glass windows to jewelry and T-shirts. The cross is probably the most common symbol of Christianity. Different cultures use different forms of the cross. The Latin cross has a longer vertical post and shorter horizontal beam. The Greek cross has horizontal and vertical beams of equal length. The Russian Orthodox cross has three horizontal bars instead of a single horizontal beam. A crucifix depicts Christ's body upon the cross.

There are other important Christian symbols. Throughout Scripture, Jesus is referred to as the Lamb of God for his role in sacrificing himself to save his people. This mirrors how Jews would sacrifice a lamb for sins during temple worship before the Second Temple in Jerusalem was destroyed in 70 CE. Scripture also calls Jesus the Good Shepherd. He knows and cares for his people, who are often referred to as his

CHRISTIAN CROSSES

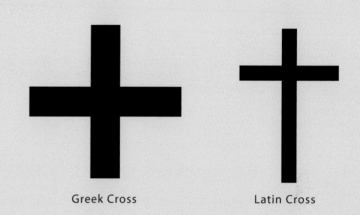

Greek Cross

Latin Cross

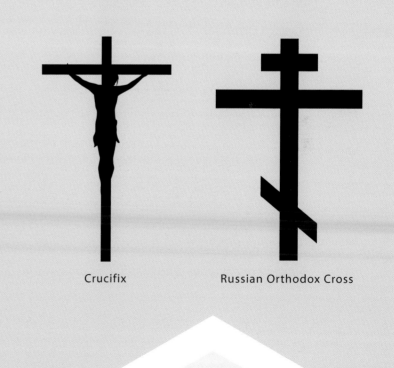

Crucifix

Russian Orthodox Cross

sheep. The Greek word for fish, *ichthys*, is spelled with the first letters in the Greek phrase that translates to "Jesus Christ, Son of God, Savior." In the early years of the church, the fish served as a secret symbol of Christianity during times of persecution.

Today's churches take all these forms and more. Some believers continue to meet in private homes, especially in countries where Christians face persecution. Others worship in elaborate churches and cathedrals that are hundreds of years old. New churches continue to be built in a range of styles. Some of the largest churches, known as megachurches, may look like shopping malls or sports arenas from the outside.

Inside, most churches today include some sort of seating. This may range from pews to theater seating. Most churches have a pulpit or stand from which the minister preaches. There is also usually a table known as the altar, which forms the center of worship in some churches. Roman Catholic and Eastern Orthodox churches are often filled with elaborate images of saints or of Christ on the cross. Protestant churches tend to include fewer decorative items, aside from a cross and candles. Some churches avoid even these Christian symbols.

Worship Leaders

Most churches have worship leaders. A worship leader generally feels he or she has been called by God to serve in the church and has often undergone training to do so at a Bible college or seminary. Afterward, the person is officially ordained, or given authority in the church. Roman Catholic, Orthodox, and Anglican churches refer to their ordained leaders as deacons, priests, and bishops. Protestant churches tend to call their ordained leaders pastors or ministers.

Different church bodies have different requirements for ministers. Roman Catholic priests, for example, must generally remain unmarried. In many church bodies, only men are ordained into the role of pastor or priest, although women may serve in other roles. These churches believe God established men as the head of the church and point to the fact that though Jesus had female followers, he ordained only male apostles. Some church bodies do not ordain their leaders. Among some Christian denominations, such as the Quakers, anyone who feels moved to speak may do so.

Some churches allow only men to be worship leaders, while others accept female worship leaders as well.

Worship Services

Christian worship services take many forms depending on denomination and location. Some churches follow a specific liturgy, or set of rituals, in each worship service. Roman Catholic and Orthodox churches tend to follow a liturgy, as do some Protestant churches. Other Protestant churches are nonliturgical, meaning they do not follow a prescribed order for their worship service.

Despite these differences, most worship services involve several common elements. With several Bible readings throughout the service, Christian worship centers on God's word. In most churches, the minister delivers an extended message about at least one of the readings. This message is known as a sermon or homily.

Prayer is also a large part of Christian worship. In prayer, Christians talk to God and trust that he hears them. Some prayers are spoken by the minister. Others, such as the Lord's Prayer, are spoken together by the congregation. During worship, believers confess they are sinners and ask

DRESSED FOR WORSHIP

In some churches, the priest or pastor wears a robe while leading worship services. This practice dates back to the Roman Empire, when everyone wore their best robes to worship. This style went out of fashion for ordinary people in the 500s. But priests continued to wear the robes while conducting worship. During the Reformation, some Protestant pastors switched to wearing the black gowns of academic professors, a practice continued in some churches today. Other Protestant worship leaders have done away with robes altogether.

God for forgiveness. The minister then offers absolution, or the promise their sins have been forgiven by God. At many churches, Christians also profess their faith using the creeds developed by the early church.

Music is another important part of worship in many churches. Eastern Orthodox Christians sing hymns unaccompanied by instruments. In many Western churches, pipe organs accompany hymn singing. Many churches have adopted more contemporary music as well, with bands playing electric guitars, keyboards, and drums.

The Sacraments

Many churches regularly practice the sacraments of baptism and Holy Communion, also called the Eucharist, during their worship services. The word *sacrament* comes from the Latin *sacramentum*, meaning "an oath of allegiance." Sacraments use ordinary elements such as water or wine to provide spiritual blessings to those who participate.

Before ascending to Heaven, Jesus told his disciples, "Go and make disciples of all nations,

TALKING TO GOD

For Christians, prayer is not limited to church services. Christians are encouraged to talk to God at any time. Jesus set the example for Christians when it came to prayer. The Bible frequently tells of Jesus going off by himself to pray, often for hours at a time. Jesus taught his disciples the Lord's Prayer, which Christians around the world continue to recite both within and outside of worship services. Many Christians also pray before meals, at the beginning and end of the day, or in times of trouble or thankfulness.

Churches have communion in different ways. In some churches, priests, ministers, or other church officials place the bread in a believer's mouth.

baptizing them in the name of the Father and of the Son and of the Holy Spirit."[1] The minister fulfills this command during baptism, repeating Jesus's words as he washes the person with water. In some churches, washing involves sprinkling water on the forehead. In others, the minister fully dunks the individual under the water. Some churches baptize babies, while others believe a person must be able to profess his or her faith before being baptized.

As Jesus celebrated his last Passover with his disciples on the night before his death, he started the practice Christians know as the Lord's Supper, Holy Communion, or Eucharist. At that meal, Jesus blessed bread and wine. He called them, "my body" and "my blood of the covenant [promise], which is poured out for many for the forgiveness of sins."[2] As Christians participate in Holy Communion today, they eat and drink bread and wine. These earthly elements are consecrated, or declared holy, by the minister, who repeats the words Jesus spoke when he instituted the sacrament. Some Christians believe the bread and wine become Jesus's body and blood. Other Christians believe Christ's body and blood are in some way present in the bread and wine. For others, the bread and wine are only symbols of Christ's body and blood, meant to remind them of Christ's sacrifice and their new hope in him.

ROMAN CATHOLIC CHRISTIANITY

One-half of all Christians in the world belong to the Roman Catholic faith, making it the largest Christian church body in the world today.[1] The word *Catholic* means "universal church." Although the Roman Catholic Church is sometimes called Catholic for short, some other church bodies, such as the Anglican and Orthodox Churches, insist that they, too, are Catholic because they maintain the essence of the universal, undivided early church. In addition, Eastern rite Catholic Churches belong to the Catholic tradition. These churches recognize the authority of the pope in Rome but follow different liturgical traditions than the Roman Catholic Church.

Pope Francis travels the world, meeting with Catholics, holding masses, and promoting Catholic values.

Popes, Bishops, and Priests

The Roman Catholic Church is headed by the pope, or bishop of Rome. *Pope* comes from the Latin *papa*, or father. Roman Catholics believe Jesus formed the office of the pope when he gave his apostle Peter a leadership role in the church. Jesus said, "You are Peter, and on this rock I will build my church."[2] Because Peter was martyred in Rome, the bishop of Rome came to be seen as his direct successor.

Popes are elected by the College of Cardinals. This is a group of approximately 120 cardinals, who are church officials ranked just below the pope, from around the world.[3] Although the cardinals can choose any Roman Catholic male to serve as pope, they typically select a cardinal for the position. The new pope chooses a new name that he uses for the rest of his life. Most popes hold their position until they die.

POPE FRANCIS

In 2013, Jorge Mario Bergoglio became the 266th Roman Catholic pope, taking the name Pope Francis.[4] Born in 1936 in Buenos Aires, Argentina, Francis studied philosophy and theology before being ordained as a priest in 1969. In 1998, Francis was named archbishop of Buenos Aires. He retained that position until being named pope in 2013. He is the first pope from South America, as well as the first from the entire Western Hemisphere. During his papacy, Francis has focused his efforts on issues such as poverty, oppression, and environmental degradation, as well as reaffirming traditional Roman Catholic values even while reaching out to people of other faiths.

Roman Catholics consider the pope to be Christ's representative on Earth. The pope is to serve as the final authority in interpreting the Bible and Church tradition. Official proclamations he makes about doctrines of faith or morals that must be believed by the whole church are called *ex cathedra*, or "from the throne." They are considered infallible, or perfect and without error. They can never be changed.

Beneath the pope and cardinals in the hierarchy of the Roman Catholic Church are bishops, priests, and deacons. Bishops oversee all the churches in a given region, known as a diocese. Bishops are overseen by archbishops, who preside over a number of dioceses. Priests serve individual churches and are sometimes assisted by deacons.

Other Roman Catholic men or women may choose to serve in the church by joining a religious order. To join an order, an individual must make three vows, or promises: poverty, chastity, and obedience. The oldest Roman Catholic order is the Order of Saint Benedict. Benedictines dedicate themselves to prayer and the study of God's word. Jesuits belong to the Society of Jesus. Their main focus is education. The brothers and sisters of the Missionaries of Charity care for the world's poorest people.

ROMAN CATHOLIC BELIEFS

Roman Catholics celebrate seven sacraments. In addition to baptism and the Eucharist, which Protestants also celebrate, Roman Catholics also observe confirmation, marriage, holy orders,

Some nuns with the Missionaries of Charity help people who have had to evacuate their homes because of natural disasters.

confession, and extreme unction. At confirmation, a believer approximately 13 years old makes a

public declaration of faith and is anointed with oil. He or she takes Communion for the first time. Those

who have been confirmed are considered members of the church. Marriage involves a commitment

made by a husband and wife to love each other as Christ loved the church. In holy orders, men who

have completed their study to enter the ministry are ordained as priests. Through ordination, a

priest's essential character is believed to be permanently changed as he receives a sacred power that

enables him to build up the church through preaching, celebrating the sacraments, and governing

Christ's people.

Confession is also known as penance or reconciliation. In this sacrament, an individual confesses

his or her sins to a priest. The priest then pronounces absolution to the sinner and assigns a penance,

or an act to make up for the sin. Penance can include saying certain prayers, denying oneself

something, or serving others in some way. Extreme unction refers to the practice of anointing the sick

with oil and praying over them. Often called the last rites, it was once performed only when a person

neared death. Today, this sacrament is more often known as anointing the sick and includes prayers

that the individual will get well.

Roman Catholic beliefs about what happens after death differ from those of most other Christian

traditions. According to Roman Catholics, some souls enter a state known as purgatory after death.

The *Catechism of the Catholic Church*, a book summarizing the beliefs of the Roman Catholic faith,

Representations of the Virgin Mary often show a halo around her head, signifying her holiness.

calls purgatory a "final purification" for those who "die in God's grace and friendship, but still imperfectly purified." This purification is referred to as a "cleansing fire" that allows believers to make up for the sins they committed on Earth so they can enter Heaven.[5] Believers still on Earth are encouraged to pray and offer works of penance on behalf of the dead in purgatory.

Roman Catholics and Saints

The Roman Catholic Church gives special recognition to saints, or individuals who lived exemplary lives on Earth and now serve as role models for other Christians. Roman

BECOMING A SAINT

In the early years of the church, there was no formal process to decide who should become a saint. It was common for various churches to honor different local martyrs. The process of canonization was established in the late 900s to recognize individuals to be added to the canon, or list, of saints who could be venerated.

The process of canonization begins when church officials investigate the deceased's reputation, virtues, writings, and miracles performed either during life or after death. During the investigation, the church assigns one person to advocate for the individual. To ensure the full truth of the person's life is exposed, another person is appointed to act as devil's advocate, looking for flaws in the deceased's contributions. If the deceased passes the investigation, the group makes a recommendation to the pope. If the pope approves, the saint may be beatified, allowing the saint to be venerated locally. The beatified person may later be canonized if there is evidence he or she has performed two miracles in response to prayers after beatification. According to estimates by the Pew Research Center, the Roman Catholic Church has canonized 10,000 saints.[6]

Catholic believers venerate the saints. They believe the saints intercede, or plead with God, on behalf of believers.

The most important saint in the Roman Catholic tradition is Jesus's mother, the Virgin Mary. Roman Catholics believe Mary was born without the stain of original sin all other humans have. They believe she did not die but that her body and soul were taken directly to Heaven at the end of her earthly life. There, she pleads with God for the salvation of human beings.

Many Roman Catholic churches include shrines to Mary and other saints. Roman Catholics often light candles and pray in front of these statues. Some saints are believed to be patrons of specific groups or places. Roman Catholics seek the prayers of these saints for protection or help with specific troubles. For example, Saint Christopher is the patron saint of travelers. Those about to leave on a trip may request that he intercede for their safety. Roman Catholics may wear medallions bearing the image of a patron saint. Some make pilgrimages to view relics, the remains of saints or the physical objects that once belonged to them.

The Authority of the Church

The doctrines of the Roman Catholic Church formed over a number of ecumenical, or church-wide, councils. The most notable include the Council of Trent, the First Vatican Council, and the Second Vatican Council. The Council of Trent was a series of meetings held between 1545 and 1563 to counteract the ideas of the Reformation. At the council, Roman Catholics rejected the Protestant doctrine of justification by faith alone. Instead, the church stressed the importance of completing good works. The council also emphasized the equal authority of scripture and church tradition. Roman Catholics continue to hold to the beliefs set out at the Council of Trent. According to Father Art, a

Roman Catholic priest in California, "We share with other Christians our reverence for Sacred Scripture, the inspired Word of God, but we have equal reverence for Sacred Tradition, the handing on to each new generation of the wider reality of all that the Church is and believes."[8]

Held from 1869 to 1870, the First Vatican Council established the infallibility of the pope concerning doctrines of faith or morals. The Second Vatican Council was held from 1962 to 1965. It led to wide reforms within the Roman Catholic Church, including allowing services—which had previously been held in Latin—to be held in modern languages. In addition, the council attempted to establish better relationships with non–Roman Catholic Christians as well as followers of other world religions. The council proclaimed that the Roman Catholic Church "rejects nothing which is true and holy in these [non-Christian] religions."[9]

EASTERN ORTHODOX CHRISTIANITY

The world's 260 million Orthodox Christians live primarily in Eastern Europe and Western Asia. Nearly 90 percent of all Orthodox Christians live in 10 countries: Russia, Ethiopia, Ukraine, Romania, Greece, Serbia, Bulgaria, Belarus, Egypt, and Georgia.[1] But a growing number of Eastern Orthodox believers can also be found in western Europe, North America, Australia, Africa, and Southeast Asia.

Patriarchs, Bishops, and Priests

In the early years after its split from the Roman Catholic Church in 1054, the Eastern Orthodox Church was headed by the Byzantine emperor, who was seen as God's representative. The emperor

Some Eastern Orthodox Christians in Bulgaria worship at the Saint Alexander Nevsky Cathedral in Sofia.

ORTHODOXY UNDER COMMUNISM

In 1917, the Bolshevik Revolution brought Communist rule to Russia, which became the Soviet Union. After World War II (1939–1945), many countries in Eastern Europe also fell under Communist control. Religion was viciously stamped out in many places because the Communist Party saw belief in God as a threat to the state. Soviet dictator Joseph Stalin once said, "The [Communist] Party cannot be neutral towards religion. It conducts an anti-religious struggle against all and any religious prejudices."[2]

In many Communist countries, Orthodox priests, bishops, monks, nuns, and even lay believers faced persecution for their beliefs. Many were sent to prisons and labor camps. Seminaries were shut down, and state governments seized church properties. Under such persecution, many Orthodox churches were forced to close. In the early 1990s, the Communist governments in the Soviet Union and Eastern Europe fell. Since then, the Eastern Orthodox Church has grown in many countries, including Russia, Ukraine, Georgia, Bulgaria, Romania, and Serbia.

performed some of the duties of a priest or bishop, including preaching sermons. In 1453, the Byzantine Empire fell. But the Eastern Orthodox Church continued.

Today, the Eastern Orthodox Church is not headed by a single authority. Instead, Eastern Orthodoxy consists of several autocephalous, or independent, churches, including the Orthodox churches of Greece, Russia, and America. The leaders of nine of these churches are known as patriarchs. The patriarchs are all considered equal, although the patriarch of Constantinople is given special honor because of that city's position as the former capital of the Byzantine Empire. But the patriarch of Constantinople does not have more power than any of the other patriarchs.

Bishops, priests, and deacons oversee preaching and ministering in the Orthodox Church. Priests can be either married or unmarried. But if they are unmarried at the time of their ordination, they must remain unmarried. If they are married and become widowed, they may not marry again. Bishops must be unmarried. At the time of their consecration, bishops are believed to receive a special gift, known as a charism, from the Holy Spirit. This gift enables the bishop to preach, teach, and celebrate the sacraments.

God and Humans

Eastern Orthodox Christians describe God in slightly different terms than other Christians. They distinguish between God's essence and his energies. God's essence is transcendent, or above all else, and thus cannot be approached by humans. But his energies fill all of creation.

Eastern Orthodox Christians also disagree with other Christians over the nature of the Holy Spirit as expressed in the Nicene Creed. This was one of the reasons for the split between the Eastern Orthodox and Roman Catholic Churches. Roman Catholics and most Protestants confess in the Nicene Creed that the Holy Spirit "proceeds [comes] from the Father and the Son."[3] But Eastern Orthodox Christians believe the Holy Spirit proceeds from the Father alone. According to Eastern Orthodox believers, the Holy Spirit can proceed only from the Father because the Father alone is the source of the Trinity.

Orthodox believers also differ from other Christians in their view of original sin and human nature. According to the Orthodox view, humans were not created perfect but rather with the potential to become perfect with God's help. Thus, Adam and Eve did not fall from perfection when they sinned.

Bartholomew began serving as patriarch of Constantinople in 1991.

They simply failed to live up to the potential to become like God. Although humans have inherited Adam and Eve's tendency to sin, they are not considered guilty of Adam and Eve's original sin.

For the Orthodox Christian, the ultimate goal in life is not justification, or being made right by God, but union with God. Through this union with God, Orthodox Christians believe they will attain *theosis*, or deification, becoming like God. The process of deification involves cooperation, or synergy, between God and the individual. Although no one can become deified without God's help, Orthodox Christians believe they must contribute to their deification through their good works. These include going to church, receiving the sacraments, praying, reading the Gospels, and obeying the commandments.

Eastern Orthodox Christians recognize the same seven sacraments as Roman Catholics, but their manner of administering some of the sacraments differs. In Eastern Orthodox baptism, an infant is fully immersed in water three times. Immediately afterward, the baby is confirmed in a ceremony sometimes called chrismation. The priest anoints the baby, making the sign of the cross over the forehead, eyes, nose, mouth, ears, breast, hands, and feet with a special ointment called chrism. Afterward, the baby receives Holy Communion. While Roman Catholic and Protestant churches use unleavened bread, or bread without yeast, for Holy Communion, Eastern Orthodox churches use leavened bread for their celebration of the Eucharist. Those partaking of the Eucharist must fast the morning before receiving Communion.

Saints and Icons

Like Roman Catholics, Eastern Orthodox believers venerate and ask the saints to pray for them. Eastern Orthodox believers give the Virgin Mary a position of honor above all saints. They give her the title, "Our All-Holy, immaculate, most blessed and glorified Lady, Mother of God and Ever-Virgin Mary."[4] Eastern Orthodox believers hold the relics of the saints in reverence and believe these items are a channel through which God works his power and healing on Earth.

A distinctive feature of any Eastern Orthodox Church is the iconostasis. This is a solid wall separating the main body of the church from the altar. This wall—along with other parts of the church—is covered with icons, or images of Christ, the saints, and angels. Orthodox believers may prostrate themselves, or lie down in adoration, in front of the icons. They also kiss the icons and burn candles in front of them to show their reverence. Orthodox believers do not see the icons as mere images but rather as glimpses of the spiritual world. According

74

An iconostasis always shows Mary with the baby Jesus to the left of the doors.

to Eastern Orthodox bishop Timothy Ware, "The icons which fill the church serve as a point of meeting between heaven and earth. As each local congregation prays . . . these visible images remind the faithful unceasingly of the invisible presence of the whole company of heaven at the Liturgy."[5]

Orthodox Christians venerate icons at home too. They may have icons in every room of their house as well as in their vehicles. At their baptism, Orthodox believers are given the name of a saint. This saint becomes their patron saint. Many believers keep an icon of their patron saint in their bedroom and request the saint's prayers daily.

ICONS AND SYMBOLISM

Icons are not meant to be realistic depictions of their subjects. Instead, they are painted according to an elaborate system of symbols that gives deeper meaning to the images. Important figures are generally painted larger than other figures. Icons may hold objects that symbolize the role they played on Earth. For example, spiritual writers often hold a scroll in their hands. A halo around a figure's head indicates the person's closeness to God. Colors add to the symbolism. Gold stands for divinity, while blue indicates truth and humility. Red can symbolize martyrdom.

PROTESTANT CHRISTIANITY

Protestant Christianity developed out of the Reformation of the 1500s. Today, more than 800 million people, or 37 percent of all Christians, belong to Protestant denominations. Approximately 20 percent of all Protestants live in the United States.[1] Other countries with a high proportion of Protestants include Nigeria, China, Brazil, and South Africa. Since the Reformation, thousands of Protestant groups have formed. Among the largest denominations are the Lutheran, Reformed, Baptist, Methodist, and Anglican churches.

Protestant Beliefs

Most Protestants share a core belief in salvation by grace alone. Protestants believe that Jesus's death on the cross paid the full price for sin. Thus, human beings need to do nothing but have faith in him to be saved.

Many Protestant churches are not as ornate as Roman Catholic or Eastern Orthodox churches. Some aim for a simpler beauty.

Protestant churches often use a plain cross as a symbol that Jesus is no longer dead.

Protestants also hold the Bible as the ultimate and only source of authority in the church. Most Protestant denominations encourage people to read and interpret the Bible for themselves rather than rely on religious authorities or the church to interpret it for them.

Protestantism has no central authority. The various Protestant denominations have set up their own systems of church governance. In some denominations, all the churches are united and led by a council of clergy or lay leaders. In others, each congregation maintains its independence with little connection to the larger church body. At the local level, congregations are led by a pastor, minister, or priest. Most Protestant ministers are permitted to marry, and some Protestant denominations ordain women.

The Lutheran Church

Martin Luther never intended to break from the Roman Catholic Church—he wanted to reform it. But his beliefs led the Roman Catholic Church to declare him a heretic, and he was officially excluded from membership. The churches of Luther and his followers came to be known by the name of the reformer. They are known as Lutheran churches.

Lutherans maintained several Roman Catholic practices, including infant baptism. But Luther translated the Bible into German so it could be read by laypeople, rather than only by the clergy and others educated in Latin. Lutherans also placed greater emphasis on the sermon message. They denied veneration of the saints and of relics.

Today, there is no single, worldwide Lutheran church. Instead, there are approximately 145 Lutheran church bodies to which individual Lutheran churches belong, supporting more than 74 million Lutherans worldwide.[2]

PERSPECTIVES

MARTIN LUTHER

Born in 1483, Martin Luther planned to become a lawyer. But after nearly being hit by a lightning strike, he became a Roman Catholic monk. As a monk, Luther spent hours each day striving to attain the perfection he thought God demanded. He went so far as to whip himself in hopes of making up for his sins. But it was never enough. As Luther later wrote, "Though I lived as a monk without reproach, I felt that I was a sinner before God with an extremely disturbed conscience. . . . I hated the righteous God who punishes sinners."[4]

But while studying Paul's letter to the Romans, Luther read, "For in the gospel the righteousness of God is revealed—a righteousness that is by faith from first to last, just as it is written: 'The righteous will live by faith.'"[5] This statement brought Luther to a realization that he did not have to—and in fact could not—do anything to be saved. Salvation came through faith in Christ, who had lived and died for him. The realization changed Luther's life: "I felt that I was altogether born again and had entered paradise itself through open gates."[6]

The Reformed Church

Luther was not the only reformer of the 1500s. John Calvin also supported reform of the Roman Catholic Church. He agreed with Luther that salvation is by grace through faith alone. But he put more emphasis on God's rule over the universe and believed God had already chosen those who would be saved and those who would go to Hell.

Calvin's theology quickly spread to several parts of Europe, including England. Over time, churches that followed Calvinist doctrine developed into the Reformed churches. Presbyterian and Congregational churches also developed out of the Reformed tradition. Today, approximately 7 percent of all Protestants belong to Reformed congregations.[3]

The Anglican Church

The Church of England, or Anglican church, was formed over a rift between England's King Henry VIII (1491–1547) and Pope Clement VII. Although Henry VIII had defended the Roman Catholic Church against Protestant reformers, he broke away from the church when the pope refused to declare his marriage invalid. Henry VIII wanted to divorce his wife Catherine because she had not given birth to a male heir to the throne. So he set up the Church of England with himself as the head.

At first, the church retained nearly all Roman Catholic practices aside from naming the pope in prayer. But other reforms after Henry's death led the Church of England in a more Protestant direction. Veneration of the saints was brought to an end, as was the practice of making pilgrimages to relics. The liturgy was also simplified. Despite these changes, the Anglican church remains closer to the practices of the Roman Catholic Church than many other Protestant denominations. Anglican churches have a similar leadership structure of bishops, priests, and deacons. In the United States and some other countries, Anglican churches are often known as Episcopal churches. Approximately 80 million people belong to Anglican and Episcopal churches.[7]

The Methodist Church

The Methodist church was founded in the 1700s as a movement to reform the Church of England. John Wesley, its founder, was an ordained Anglican priest. Wesley emphasized worshipping God

The African Methodist Episcopal Church (AME) is a branch of the Methodist denomination. Some AME churches have choirs.

and studying the Bible, as well as maintaining a personal relationship with God. Methodists strive to achieve perfect love through the help of the Holy Spirit. In some Methodist churches, services are conducted by lay preachers rather than ordained ministers.

Today, there are more than 80 million Methodist Christians throughout the world.[8] Methodists can be found across much of Europe as well as in the United States and Canada. Australia, Latin America, India, and many parts of Africa also have Methodist churches.

The Baptist Church

The Baptist church also has its roots in the Church of England. Baptists separated from the Church of England in the 1600s to establish their own forms of worship. They eliminated many of the liturgical practices of the Anglican church. Baptist churches reject infant baptism. Instead, they baptize only those who have professed their faith. Baptists baptize by fully immersing the body in water rather than pouring water over the forehead.

Baptists might use lakes, rivers, or even oceans for baptisms.

THE BLACK CHURCH

In the late 1700s and early 1800s, both enslaved and free African Americans started their own congregations in the United States. These churches were both led and attended by black worshippers. Although enslaved people were generally not permitted to leave slaveholders' lands, many did so anyway, risking punishment or even death to attend services. Black churches often faced persecution, including the burning of their buildings and beating or killing of their leaders. Before the Civil War (1861–1865), the black church was active in the abolition, or antislavery, movement. Black churches also played an important role in the civil rights movement of the 1960s. Martin Luther King Jr., the leader of that movement, was a Baptist minister.

Black churches today often focus on the experience and heritage of being an African American. Many black churches are actively involved in movements to end racial discrimination and oppression. According to researcher Marilyn Mellowes, "The black church continues to offer affirmation and dignity to people still searching for equality and justice, still willing to reach out for a more inclusive, embracing tomorrow."[10]

The black church includes a diversity of denominations. The National Baptist Convention of the USA is the largest association of black Baptist churches in the United States, with nearly 8.5 million members.[11] The African Methodist Episcopal Church has 3.5 million members.[12]

Today, Baptists make up one of the largest Protestant denominations in the world. More than 110 million people identify as Baptist, many of them in the United States.[9] There are also many Baptists in the Democratic Republic of the Congo, Nigeria, and other parts of Africa.

RADICAL CHRISTIANITY AND LEGALISM

In the 2010s, a new movement known as Radical Christianity began to grow. This movement sought to counteract the complacency—or lack of action—on the part of many Christians. It encouraged them to change their lives for Christ. For some believers, this meant going so far as to sell everything they owned and become missionaries. While some Christians applauded this movement, others rejected it as a form of legalism, which seeks to follow certain rules or complete certain actions to prove one's faith. According to Jonathan Hollingsworth, who gave away his possessions to become a missionary in Africa, his move was an attempt to "prove to God that I was really dedicated to Him."[13] Hollingsworth now realizes people should serve God not out of guilt but out of love.

Christian Movements

In addition to belonging to different denominations, some Christians also hold to specific movements within Christianity. The Pentecostal movement has emerged in some Protestant denominations. Pentecostals believe that after coming to faith, Christians receive the baptism of the Holy Spirit, through which they are given spiritual gifts. These gifts can include the ability to heal or to prophesy—sharing messages received directly from God. The ability to speak in tongues, or spiritual languages unknown to anyone on Earth, is also considered a gift of the Spirit.

Pentecostal worship is often emotional and can involve the whole body as people raise their arms, applaud, and cheer. Worship services tend to be informal rather than highly structured. They focus on interaction with the Holy Spirit. Today, the Assemblies of God is the largest Pentecostal denomination in the world, with millions of followers worldwide. Many Pentecostals can be found in the United States, Latin America, South Korea, and parts of Africa.

Christians who are not part of Pentecostal denominations but who follow at least some Pentecostal practices are known as charismatics. Charismatic believers can be found among Roman Catholic, Eastern Orthodox, and some Protestant denominations. Like Pentecostals, charismatics may emphasize spiritual gifts and display strong emotion in worship.

The evangelical movement plays a role in nearly every Protestant denomination. Evangelical Christians stress the importance of the experience of accepting Christ as Lord and Savior, often known as being born again. Evangelicals also emphasize the need for a personal relationship with Christ. The focus of evangelical churches is evangelism, or sharing the Gospel with non-Christians.

TODAY AND THE FUTURE

Christians have made numerous contributions to social welfare, the arts, and sciences. But Christianity also faces several challenges both within the church and around the world. Since the time of the Reformation, many Christians have debated the roles of science and faith. In the 1500s, scientists Nicholas Copernicus and Galileo Galilei proved that the sun, and not the earth, was at the center of the universe. This challenged many people's views that God had created humanity at the center of his universe.

People continued to question the role of God as science further developed. Perhaps the greatest challenge came in 1859 with the publication of Charles Darwin's *On the Origin of Species*. This book explained Darwin's theory of evolution, or the idea that all living creatures slowly developed, or evolved, from a common ancestor. Darwin's theory led many to question the biblical account of creation

Charles Darwin's study of finches on the isolated Galápagos Islands in Ecuador inspired his ideas about evolution.

as presented in Genesis, the first book of the Bible. Genesis describes how God created the world in six days, simply by his command.

Debates over the role of God and evolution in the creation of the world continue today. Some Christians reject the theory of evolution as unbiblical. They hold to a literal interpretation of a six-day creation as described in Genesis. During those days approximately 10,000 years ago, God created all species on Earth. Other Christians do not believe that evolution and creation are in conflict. Some believe the days in Genesis refer not to literal days but to longer periods of time. Others believe God set in motion the cosmic reaction that created the world but then stepped back and allowed evolution to take over. Others reject God's role entirely and insist that life formed and evolved through a chain of events that can be fully explained using science.

SEXUAL ABUSE SCANDAL

In the early 2000s, the *Boston Globe* published a series of reports exposing a decades-long problem in the Roman Catholic Church: sexual abuse of minors by members of the clergy. The reports showed 4,400 US priests abused children from 1950 to 2002.[1] In response to the reports, the Roman Catholic Church established the National Review Board. This board created new policies and procedures and required training programs for those who work with children. In more recent years, some Christians have contended there is also a sexual abuse problem within the Anglican church, as well as within some fundamentalist evangelical churches.

HOMOSEXUALITY AND THE EPISCOPAL CHURCH

The issue of homosexuality has perhaps been debated most dramatically and publicly within the Episcopal church. In 2003, the Episcopal Church in the United States (ECUS) consecrated Gene Robinson as its first openly gay bishop. The ECUS also affirmed same-sex marriages in 2015. These events led to a fierce debate among Episcopal churches around the world. In 2016, the worldwide Anglican church officially imposed penalties banning the ECUS from voting on key doctrinal issues for three years. Similar penalties were imposed against the Anglican Church in Scotland when it also began to allow same-sex marriages in 2017.

Some Episcopal churches, primarily in Africa, thought more-drastic measures should be taken against the US and Scottish churches. In a September 2017 open letter to the Anglican church, Archbishop Nicholas Okoh of Nigeria stated the disagreement could lead to "the next great Reformation. In our day also there is broken fellowship, over homosexual practice, same-sex marriage, and the blurring of gender identity. . . . all of which contradict fundamental biblical understandings of marriage and human identity."[2]

Christians and Homosexuality

Among the most difficult debates within the Christian church today is over homosexuality, especially in relation to same-sex marriage and the ordination of homosexual clergy. The majority of Christian churches consider homosexuality a sin. This does not mean these churches do not welcome homosexual members. Many churches see homosexuality as a sin like any other sin. They try to love homosexuals, just as they are to love all sinners, following Jesus's example. Although some Christians do speak hatefully against homosexuals, most Christians do not consider this a Christian way to think or behave. But because many Christian churches see homosexuality as a sin, they do not allow same-sex marriages. Churches that reject same-sex marriage include the Roman Catholic, Baptist,

Conflicting views of homosexuality have led to tensions within denominations as they decide whether to accept it.

and Methodist churches, some Lutheran churches and other Protestant denominations, and Eastern Orthodox churches. These churches hold that the Bible establishes marriage as a union between a man and a woman. Most of these denominations also refuse the ordination of openly homosexual individuals to the ministry.

Since the 1960s, however, some churches have rejected the idea that homosexuality is a sin. Churches such as the Unitarian Universalists, United Church of Christ, and Metropolitan Community Churches perform same-sex marriages and ordain homosexual clergy. In other denominations, such as the Presbyterian Church and the Evangelical Lutheran Church of America, the decision of whether to conduct same-sex marriages or ordain openly homosexual ministers is left to individual congregations.

Christian Unity

Many of today's Christians feel the divisions between different denominations represent a failure to live up to the biblical ideal of a united worldwide church. Many churches have committed themselves to the ecumenical, or church-wide, movement to establish unity within the Christian church.

The World Council of Churches (WCC) was formed in 1948 to oversee the ecumenical movement. The WCC identifies itself as "a fellowship of churches which confess the Lord Jesus Christ as God and Saviour according to the scriptures, and therefore seek to fulfill together their common calling to the glory of one God, Father, Son, and Holy Spirit."[3] Today the organization encompasses nearly 350 Orthodox, Anglican, Baptist, Lutheran,

PERSPECTIVES

FAITH AND ART

Makoto Fujimura is an artist, author, and speaker who grew up in both the United States and Japan. He uses a Japanese style of creating art called *nihonga*. It uses hand-mixed mineral paints, animal glue, and metals applied to a canvas that might be silk, paper, or another material. It takes a long time to master this art.

Fujimura believes art began with God, who created all things. He considers creating art an act of worship. The paintings he makes are largely abstract. He uses the best-quality materials he can, even when working with gold. In 2011, one publishing company celebrated the 400th anniversary of the King James Version of the Bible. Fujimura created art to go along with the four Gospels. He made beautiful letters to start each chapter and added designs down the margins of the text.

Fujimura talks about how Christians often do not support the arts today. He noted how the Gospels haven't been accompanied by art in a long time because "the fragmentation between the church and the arts, particularly the visual arts, has been so profound."[4] He hopes to mend that divide with his work.

THE CHURCH AND MUSIC

Christianity has had a strong impact on the development of music. In the 1700s, the melodies of both traditional European folk songs and African American spirituals were incorporated into many hymns. The rhythms of these hymns later influenced the development of blues, gospel, jazz, rock, and even rap music. Many of the songs played by modern orchestras were written by Christian composers to be used in the church. Among such classical pieces are George Frideric Handel's *Messiah* and Johann Sebastian Bach's *Christmas Oratorio*.

Methodist, Reformed, and other church bodies from 110 countries.[5]

Christianity and Culture

Despite its challenges, Christianity has made important cultural and scientific contributions to the world. In the Middle Ages, belief in God as the creator sparked interest in scientific investigation of his creation. From the 400s to the late 1700s, the Roman Catholic Church was among the leading sources of funding for scientific research and still funds research today. Roman Catholic monks were at the forefront of science and published thousands of papers about scientific topics. The study of modern genetics traces its origins to Austrian monk Gregor Mendel's work with plants.

Christianity has also made important contributions to the arts. During the Renaissance (approximately 1400–1600) especially, the church was often a leading patron of the arts. The church commissioned many masterpieces, including Michelangelo's painting of the Sistine Chapel's ceiling in Rome. Some of the most important works of art of the past 2,000 years reflect biblical themes. Christian architecture has also influenced the form and style of buildings around the world.

Love Your Neighbor

In addition to contributing to culture, Christians are dedicated to serving people both within and outside of the church. Since its earliest days, the church has been dedicated to caring for the vulnerable, including widows, orphans, and the disabled. Today, Christian organizations are at the forefront of movements for social justice and poverty relief around the world. For example, as part of its mission to increase church unity, the WCC undertakes several social service projects. The organization is active in mission work, disaster and poverty relief, and racial and economic justice. The Christian organization Compassion International provides medical care, food, education, and the Gospel to children in some of the world's poorest countries. International Justice Mission (IJM) works to free those exploited by slavery, international sex trafficking, and other injustices. According to the IJM's mission statement, the organization is "inspired by God's call to love all people and seek justice."[6] Other Christian organizations dedicated to providing services to the poor, oppressed, and vulnerable include Bread for the World, International Orthodox Charities, Catholic Relief Services, and World Vision.

At the local level, many Christian churches serve their communities through food pantries, homeless shelters, free clinics, and other programs to help those struggling with poverty and oppression. Many churches also operate schools and universities to provide educational opportunities. All of these activities come from the biblical command to "love your neighbor as yourself."[7]

Catholics in the Philippines teamed up with EcoWaste Coalition to try to reduce trash in the country.

Christian Stewards

Christians consider themselves to be stewards, or caretakers, of God's creation. In recent years, many Christians have been at the forefront of environmental protection efforts. After being named pope in 2013, Pope Francis made environmental protection a key cause of his papacy. "God gave us a bountiful garden," the pope said in a 2016 statement, "but we have turned it into a polluted wasteland of debris, desolation, and filth."[8] He called the destruction of the earth by man a sin and warned that because of humans, "thousands of species will no longer give glory to God by their very existence."[9] The pope called on all Christians to care for the environment. He pointed out that environmental destruction has the greatest impact on the poor, whom the church is also called to care for.

Care for the environment crosses the boundaries between Christian groups. Like Pope Francis, Orthodox Christian leader Patriarch Bartholomew called mistreating the environment a sin. "If human beings were to treat one another's personal property the way they treat the natural environment,

we would view that behavior as anti-social and illegal," he said. "When will we learn that to commit

a crime against the natural world is also a sin?"[10] In September 2017, Pope Francis and Patriarch

Bartholomew issued a joint appeal for environmental protection.

Christian organizations around the world have heeded the call to care for the environment. Target

Earth is a Christian environmental organization that works to feed the hungry, save endangered

animals, and replant forests. The charity A Rocha provides water filters to communities in Uganda,

helps protect Asian elephants, and supports scientific research, among other projects. The Evangelical

Environmental Network promotes policies that protect the environment.

Now and Into the Future

Christianity remains an active force in the world. Throughout its 2,000-year history, Christianity has

faced both challenges and triumphs in sharing its message with the world. A religion that began

with the birth of Jesus in the small town of Bethlehem has spread to every country of the world. As

Christians live on Earth, they look to serve God and their neighbors. But they also look forward to a

day when they will live forever in the glory of Heaven. As they wait for that day, Christians continue

to proclaim Jesus's love. And they declare the joyous Easter message: "Christ has risen. He has truly

risen!"[11]

ESSENTIAL FACTS

DATE FOUNDED

Christianity began in the 30s CE.

BASIC BELIEFS

Christians believe God is triune, or one God in three persons—Father, Son, and Holy Spirit. They believe Jesus Christ is both true God and true man and took on human form to live a perfect life and to die on the cross for the sins of all people. Christians trust that Jesus rose from the dead, giving them the promise that they will one day also rise from the dead and live eternally with God. The greatest commandments Jesus left with his followers were to love God and to love your neighbor.

IMPORTANT HOLIDAYS AND EVENTS

- Christmas, December 25, which marks the birth of Jesus
- Lent, a 40-day period of reflection and repentance before Easter
- Easter, a celebration held in spring to mark the resurrection of Jesus from the dead
- Pentecost, 50 days after Easter, which marks the coming of the Holy Spirit to believers

FAITH LEADERS

- Jesus the Messiah came to take away the sins of the world. Belief in him is the foundation of Christianity.

- Peter was one of Jesus's apostles. Jesus gave him the commission to lead the church.

- Paul was a Jew who originally persecuted Christians. After a conversion experience, he became a leading Christian missionary and authored many letters to the early church that are preserved in the New Testament.

- Constantine was a Roman emperor who legalized Christianity.

- Martin Luther was a German monk who sparked the Protestant Reformation with his desires to reform the Roman Catholic Church.

- Pope Francis became the head of the Roman Catholic Church in 2013.

NUMBER OF PEOPLE WHO PRACTICE CHRISTIANITY

Christianity is the largest religion with approximately 2.3 billion followers (approximately 1 billion are Roman Catholic, 800 million are Protestant, and 260 million are Orthodox).

QUOTE

"The cornerstone of the Christian faith is the resurrection of Christ. If there was no resurrection, there would be no Christianity. . . . We have different theologies and different liturgies, but there is one thing that unites all the Christians around the world and that is Christ is risen."

—*Enock De Assis, Presbyterian pastor*

GLOSSARY

ADULTERY
Sex between a married person and someone who is not that person's wife or husband.

ANGEL
A spiritual being that is a messenger of God.

BLASPHEMY
Words or actions that show disrespect, ridicule, or contempt for God.

CLERGY
People ordained to lead worship or perform other church duties.

DENOMINATION
A religious body made up of many individual congregations that share the same beliefs and name.

EQUINOX
The date in spring and in fall when the sun crosses the equator, resulting in equal hours of daylight and darkness.

FAST
A period of time during which a person does not eat at all or does not eat specific foods.

GRACE
Help given from God to people who don't deserve it.

HERESY
A belief that contradicts those stated by the church.

INDIGENOUS
Originating in or native to a place.

LAY
Having to do with people who are not ordained members of the clergy.

MONK
A man who has joined a religious order and has taken vows of poverty, chastity, and obedience.

PATRON

A guardian.

PILGRIMAGE

A long journey to a sacred place to
show devotion.

PROFESS

To declare belief in something.

SCRIPTURE

A holy and authoritative collection
of writings.

SEMINARY

A theological college for the training of
priests or ministers.

SHRINE

An area or monument dedicated to a
particular saint and often containing a statue,
image, or object depicting that saint.

THEOLOGIAN

One who studies theology.

THEOLOGY

The study of God and religion or the
doctrines that make up a specific religion.

VIRGIN

A person who has never had
sexual intercourse.

ADDITIONAL RESOURCES

SELECTED BIBLIOGRAPHY

Bowden, John, ed. *Encyclopedia of Christianity*. New York: Oxford UP, 2005. Print.

Brodd, Jeffrey, et al., eds. *Invitation to World Religions*. 2nd ed. New York: Oxford UP, 2016. Print.

Esposito, John L., et al. *World Religions Today*. 3rd ed. New York: Oxford UP, 2009. Print.

Wainwright, Geoffrey, and Karen B. Westerfield Tucker, eds. *The Oxford History of Christian Worship*. New York: Oxford UP, 2006. Print.

Ware, Timothy. *The Orthodox Church*. New York: Penguin, 1993. Print.

FURTHER READINGS

Capaccio, George. *Religion in Colonial America*. New York: Cavendish Square, 2015. Print.

Enzo, George. *The Reformation*. New York: Cavendish Square, 2017. Print.

Lanser, Amanda. *Pope Francis: Spiritual Leader and Voice of the Poor*. Minneapolis: Abdo, 2013. Print.

ONLINE RESOURCES

To learn more about Christianity, visit **abdobooklinks.com**. These links are routinely monitored and updated to provide the most current information available.

MORE INFORMATION

For more information on this subject, contact or visit the following organizations:

MUSEUM OF THE BIBLE

400 Fourth Street SW
Washington, DC 20024
855-554-5300
museumofthebible.org

The Museum of the Bible offers exhibits reflecting upon the impact of the Bible in America and the world.

THE VATICAN MUSEUMS

Viale Vaticano
00165 Rome
+39 06 69884676
museivaticani.va/content/museivaticani/en.html

The Vatican Museums display works of art and history collected by popes throughout history.

SOURCE NOTES

Chapter 1. He Is Risen

1. "Easter in Greece!" *Greece All Time Classic*. GNTO, 2017. Web. 9 Mar. 2018.

2. "Global Christianity—A Report on the Size and Distribution of the World's Christian Population." *Pew Research Center*. Pew Research Center, 19 Dec. 2011. Web. 9 Mar. 2018.

3. "Easter Traditions." *PolAmJournal. com*. Polish American Journal, 2018. Web. 9 Mar. 2018.

4. "Masses with the Pope at the Vatican." *Papal Audience with Pope Francis*. Prefecture of the Papal Household, n.d. Web. 9 Mar. 2018.

5. "Los Angeles Celebrates Sunrise Easter Services at the Hollywood Bowl, Forum." *Beverly Hills Courier*. BH Courier, 2018. Web. 9 Mar. 2018.

6. Carol Kuruvilla. "'The Passion of the Christ' Actor Promises Sequel to Be 'Biggest Film in History.'" *Huffington Post*. Huffington Post, 2 Feb. 2018. Web. 9 Mar. 2018.

7. Catherine Shoard. "Mel Gibson to Focus on Resurrection for Passion of the Christ 2." *Guardian*. Guardian, 10 June 2016. Web. 9 Mar. 2018.

Chapter 2. In the Beginning

1. *Holy Bible*. New International Version, Zondervan, 2011. Galatians 1:13–14.

2. *Holy Bible*, Galatians 1:11–12.

3. E. P. Sanders. "Saint Paul, the Apostle." *Encyclopædia Britannica*. Encyclopædia Britannica, 2018. Web. 9 Mar. 2018.

4. "The Reasons for the Holocaust." *History of the Holocaust (Shoah): Holocaust: A Call to Conscience*. Projetaladin.org, n.d. Web. 9 Mar. 2018.

Chapter 3. Christianity around the World

1. Conrad Hackett. "Christians Remain World's Largest Religious Group, but They Are Declining in Europe." *FacTank*. Pew Research Center, 5 Apr. 2017. Web. 9 Mar. 2018.

2. "Global Christianity—A Report on the Size and Distribution of the World's Christian Population." *Pew Research Center: Religion & Public Life*. Pew Research Center, 19 Dec. 2011. Web. 9 Mar. 2018.

3. "Guide: Christians in the Middle East." *BBC News*. BBC, 11 Oct. 2011. Web. 9 Mar. 2018.

4. "Global Christianity."

5. "Global Christianity."

6. "Global Christianity."

7. Phillip Connor. "6 Facts about South Korea's Growing Christian Population." *FacTank*. Pew Research Center, 12 Aug. 2014. Web. 9 Mar. 2018.

8. Matthew Bell. "The Biggest Megachurch on Earth and South Korea's 'Crisis of Evangelism.'" *PRI*. PRI, 1 May 2017. Web. 9 Mar. 2018.

9. "Global Christianity."

10. "Regional Distributions of Christians." *Pew Research Center: Religion & Public Life*. Pew Research Center, 19 Dec. 2011. Web. 9 Mar. 2018.

11. "Global Christianity."

12. "Many Countries Favor Specific Religions, Officially or Unofficially." *Pew Research Center: Religion & Public Life*. Pew Research Center, 3 Oct. 2017. Web. 9 Mar. 2018.

13. "Many Countries Favor Specific Religions."

14. "Religion in Latin America." *Pew Research Center: Religion & Pubic Life*. Pew Research Center, 13 Nov. 2014. Web. 9 Mar. 2018.

15. "Religious Landscape Study: Religions." *Pew Research Center: Religion & Pubic Life*. Pew Research Center, 2018. Web. 9 Mar. 2018.

16. "America's Changing Religious Landscape." *Pew Research Center: Religion & Pubic Life*. Pew Research Center, 12 May 2015. Web. 9 Mar. 2018.

Chapter 4. Christian Beliefs

1. "Why Bible Translation?" *Wycliffe*. Wycliffe Bible Translators, 2017. Web. 9 Mar. 2018.

2. *Holy Bible*. New International Version, Zondervan, 2011. 1 Chron. 21:1–16.

3. *Holy Bible*, Matthew 22:37–39.

4. *Holy Bible*, Matthew 5:21–22.

5. *Holy Bible*, Luke 15:1–7.

6. *Holy Bible*, Hebrews 11:1.

Chapter 5. Worship and Praise

1. *Holy Bible*. New International Version, Zondervan, 2011. Matthew 28:19.

2. *Holy Bible*, Matthew 26:26–28.

Chapter 6. Roman Catholic Christianity

1. "Global Christianity—A Report on the Size and Distribution of the World's Christian Population." *Pew Research Center: Religion & Public Life*. Pew Research Center, 19 Dec. 2011. Web. 9 Mar. 2018.

2. *Holy Bible*. New International Version, Zondervan, 2011. Matthew 16:18.

3. "How Is a New Pope Chosen?" *United States Conference of Catholic Bishops*. United States Conference of Catholic Bishops, 2018. Web. 9 Mar. 2018.

4. "Pope Francis Fast Facts." *CNN World*. CNN, 4 Dec. 2017. Web. 9 Mar. 2018.

SOURCE NOTES CONTINUED

5. "Catechism of the Catholic Church." *La Santa Sede Francesco*. Libreria Deitrice Vaticana, n.d. Web. 9 Mar. 2018.

6. Michael Lipka and Tim Townsend. "Papal Saints: Once a Given, Now Extremely Rare." *FacTank*. Pew Research Center, 24 Apr. 2014. Web. 9 Mar. 2018.

7. "Vatican Fast Facts." *CNN World*. CNN, 8 Apr. 2017. Web. 9 Mar. 2018.

8. Jeffrey Brodd, et al. *Invitation to World Religions*. 2nd ed. New York: Oxford UP, 2016. Print. 424–425.

9. Dr. Jeff Mirus. "Vatican II on Non-Christian Religions." *Catholic Culture.org*. Trinity Communications, 20 July 2010. Web. 9 Mar. 2018.

Chapter 7. Eastern Orthodox Christianity

1. Conrad Hackett and Brian Grim. "Global Christianity: A Report on the Size and Distribution of the World's Christian Population." Pew Research Center's Forum on Religion & Public Life, 2011. 31. PDF. *Pew Research Center*, Dec. 2011. Web. 9 Mar. 2018.

2. Timothy Ware. *The Orthodox Church*. New York: Penguin, 1993. Print. 145.

3. Ware, *The Orthodox Church*, 50.

4. Ware, *The Orthodox Church*, 256–257.

5. Ware, *The Orthodox Church*, 271.

Chapter 8. Protestant Christianity

1. Conrad Hackett and Brian Grim. "Global Christianity: A Report on the Size and Distribution of the World's Christian Population." Pew Research Center's Forum on Religion & Public Life, 2011. 27. PDF. *Pew Research Center*, Dec. 2011. Web. 9 Mar. 2018.

2. "More than 74 Million Members in LWF's 145 Churches." *Lutheran World Federation*. Lutheran World Federation, 30 Aug. 2016. Web. 9 Mar. 2018.

3. Hackett and Grim, "Global Christianity," 70.

4. Lewis Spitz, ed. *Luther's Works*. Vol. 34. Philadelphia: Fortress Press, 1960. Print. 337–338.

5. *Holy Bible*. New International Version, Zondervan, 2011. Romans 1:17.

6. Jeffrey David Oldham. "Martin Luther." *Stanford Theory Group*. Stanford University, 9 Oct. 2009. Web. 9 Mar. 2018.

7. "The Anglican Communion." *Episcopal Church*. Domestic and Foreign Missionary Society, 2018. Web. 9 Mar. 2018.

8. "Member Churches: Our World Wide Church Family." *World Methodist Council*. World Methodist Council, n.d. Web. 9 Mar. 2018.

9. "The Baptists: Our Beliefs and Practices." *Old Harbour Bay Circuit of Baptist Churches*. Old Harbour Bay Circuit of Baptist Churches, 2018. Web. 9 Mar. 2018.

10. Marilyn Mellowes. "The Black Church." *God in America*. PBS, 2012. Web. 9 Mar. 2018.

11. "National Baptist Convention of the United States of America, Inc." *Encyclopædia Britannica*. Encyclopædia Britannica, 2018. Web. 9 Mar. 2018.

12. "Historically African American Denominations." *Faith Communities Today*. Hartford Seminary, 2018. Web. 9 Mar. 2018.

13. Heather Sells. "Radical for Jesus a New Kind of Legalism?" *CBN News*. CBN News, 1 July 2015. Web. 9 Mar. 2018.

Chapter 9. Today and the Future

1. Martha Quillin. "Hollywood, Here's Some Advice on Your Sex-Abuse Scandals—From the Catholic Church." *News & Observer*. News & Observer, 2 Nov. 2017. Web. 9 Mar. 2018.

2. Harriet Sherwood. "Scottish Anglican Church Faces Sanctions Over Vote to Allow Same-Sex Marriage." *Guardian*. Guardian, 27 Sept. 2017. Web. 9 Mar. 2018.

3. "What Is the World Council of Churches?" *World Council of Churches*. World Council of Churches, 2018. Web. 9 Mar. 2018.

4. "Inspire Your Budding Artist: An Interview with Makoto Fujimura." *HSLDA*. HSLDA, 17 June 2016. Web. 9 Mar. 2018.

5. "What Is the World Council of Churches?"

6. "Justice Is Our Middle Name." *International Justice Mission*. International Justice Mission, 2018. Web. 9 Mar. 2018.

7. *Holy Bible*. New International Version, Zondervan, 2011. Mark 12:31

8. Crispian Balmer. "Pope Urges Christians to Save Planet from 'Debris, Desolation and Filth.'" *Reuters*. Reuters, 1 Sept. 2016. Web. 9 Mar. 2018.

9. Josephine McKenna. "Pope Francis Says Destroying the Environment Is a Sin." *Guardian*. Guardian, 1 Sept. 2016. Web. 9 Mar. 2018.

10. Patriarch Bartholomew. "Environmental Justice and Peace." *Ecumenical Patriarchate*. Ecumenical Patriarchate of Constantinople, 2018. Web. 9 Mar. 2018.

11. "Easter in Greece!" *Greece All Time Classic*. GNTO, 2017. Web. 9 Mar. 2018.

INDEX

ABOUT THE AUTHOR

Valerie Bodden is the author of more than 250 nonfiction children's books. Her books have received critical acclaim from *School Library Journal*, *Booklist*, *Children's Literature*, *ForeWord Magazine*, *Horn Book Guide*, *VOYA*, and *Library Media Connection*. Valerie lives in Wisconsin with her husband, four children, one dog, two cats, a growing collection of fish, and miscellaneous bugs that her children have "rescued" from the outdoors. Her Christian faith is an important part of her life.